50 Freshly Baked Pies

By: Kelly Johnson

Table of Contents

- Classic Apple Pie
- Cherry Pie
- Pumpkin Pie
- Lemon Meringue Pie
- Blueberry Pie
- Pecan Pie
- Peach Pie
- Chocolate Cream Pie
- Key Lime Pie
- Strawberry Rhubarb Pie
- Sweet Potato Pie
- Coconut Cream Pie
- Banana Cream Pie
- Mixed Berry Pie
- Apple Cranberry Pie
- Caramel Pecan Pie
- Maple Walnut Pie
- Pear Almond Pie
- Rhubarb Pie
- Buttermilk Pie
- Chess Pie
- Maple Pecan Pie
- Lemon Custard Pie
- S'mores Pie
- Hazelnut Chocolate Pie
- Plum Pie
- Pineapple Coconut Pie
- Blackberry Pie
- Bourbon Pecan Pie
- Chocolate Chip Pie
- Bourbon Peach Pie
- Almond Joy Pie
- Pear Ginger Pie
- Raspberry Pie
- Triple Berry Pie

- Apricot Pie
- Key Lime Coconut Pie
- Apricot Almond Pie
- Sweet Lemon Pie
- Gingerbread Pie
- Chocolate Pudding Pie
- Baked Custard Pie
- Walnut Pie
- Apple Butter Pie
- Cider Pie
- Caramel Apple Pie
- Mincemeat Pie
- Raspberry Almond Pie
- Pumpkin Pecan Pie
- Lemon Blueberry Pie

Classic Apple Pie

Ingredients:

- 6-7 medium apples (Granny Smith or Honeycrisp are great options)
- 1 cup granulated sugar
- 2 tbsp all-purpose flour
- 1 tsp ground cinnamon
- 1/4 tsp ground nutmeg
- 1 tbsp lemon juice
- 2 tbsp butter, cut into small pieces
- 1 egg (for egg wash)
- 1 package pie crust (or homemade)

Instructions:

1. Preheat oven to 425°F (220°C).
2. Peel, core, and slice the apples. Place them in a large mixing bowl.
3. Add sugar, flour, cinnamon, nutmeg, and lemon juice to the apples. Toss to coat evenly.
4. Roll out the pie crust and place one layer in a pie pan.
5. Pour the apple mixture into the crust, spreading evenly.
6. Dot the top with butter and cover with the second pie crust. Seal the edges and make slits in the top for ventilation.
7. Brush the top crust with a beaten egg for a golden finish.
8. Bake for 45-50 minutes, until the crust is golden and the filling is bubbling.
9. Let cool before serving.

Cherry Pie

Ingredients:

- 4 cups fresh or frozen cherries
- 1 cup granulated sugar
- 2 tbsp cornstarch
- 1 tbsp lemon juice
- 1/4 tsp almond extract (optional)
- 1 tbsp butter
- 1 package pie crust (or homemade)

Instructions:

1. Preheat oven to 425°F (220°C).
2. In a saucepan, combine the cherries, sugar, cornstarch, and lemon juice. Cook over medium heat, stirring until the mixture thickens and boils.
3. Remove from heat and stir in almond extract (if using).
4. Roll out the bottom pie crust and place it in a pie dish.
5. Pour the cherry filling into the crust and dot with butter.
6. Cover with the top crust, sealing the edges and cutting slits for ventilation.
7. Bake for 40-45 minutes until the crust is golden brown.
8. Let cool before serving.

Pumpkin Pie

Ingredients:

- 1 can (15 oz) pumpkin puree
- 1 cup heavy cream
- 2 large eggs
- 3/4 cup granulated sugar
- 1 tsp ground cinnamon
- 1/2 tsp ground ginger
- 1/4 tsp ground nutmeg
- 1/4 tsp salt
- 1 tsp vanilla extract
- 1 package pie crust (or homemade)

Instructions:

1. Preheat oven to 425°F (220°C).
2. In a large bowl, whisk together the pumpkin puree, cream, eggs, sugar, cinnamon, ginger, nutmeg, salt, and vanilla until smooth.
3. Pour the mixture into the prepared pie crust.
4. Bake for 15 minutes at 425°F, then reduce temperature to 350°F (175°C) and bake for an additional 40-45 minutes, or until the filling is set.
5. Let cool completely before serving.

Lemon Meringue Pie

Ingredients:

- 1 pie crust (pre-baked or homemade)
- 1 cup granulated sugar
- 2 tbsp cornstarch
- 1/4 tsp salt
- 1 1/2 cups water
- 3 large egg yolks (reserve the whites for meringue)
- 1/2 cup fresh lemon juice
- 1 tbsp lemon zest
- 2 tbsp butter
- 1/4 tsp cream of tartar
- 1/2 cup granulated sugar (for meringue)
- 1 tsp vanilla extract

Instructions:

1. Preheat oven to 350°F (175°C).
2. In a saucepan, combine sugar, cornstarch, and salt. Gradually whisk in water, and cook over medium heat until the mixture thickens.
3. Whisk in egg yolks, lemon juice, lemon zest, and butter. Cook for another 2 minutes.
4. Pour the lemon filling into the pre-baked pie crust.
5. In a clean bowl, beat the egg whites with cream of tartar until soft peaks form. Gradually add sugar and beat until stiff peaks form.
6. Spread the meringue over the lemon filling, sealing the edges.
7. Bake for 10-12 minutes, or until the meringue is golden brown.
8. Let cool completely before serving.

Blueberry Pie

Ingredients:

- 4 cups fresh or frozen blueberries
- 3/4 cup granulated sugar
- 2 tbsp cornstarch
- 1/4 tsp ground cinnamon
- 1 tbsp lemon juice
- 1 package pie crust (or homemade)

Instructions:

1. Preheat oven to 375°F (190°C).
2. In a large bowl, combine blueberries, sugar, cornstarch, cinnamon, and lemon juice. Stir gently.
3. Roll out the bottom crust and place it in a pie dish.
4. Pour the blueberry mixture into the pie crust.
5. Cover with the top crust, sealing the edges and cutting slits for ventilation.
6. Bake for 45-50 minutes until the crust is golden and the filling is bubbling.
7. Let cool before serving.

Pecan Pie

Ingredients:

- 1 1/2 cups pecans
- 3/4 cup light corn syrup
- 1/2 cup granulated sugar
- 3 large eggs
- 1/4 tsp salt
- 1 tsp vanilla extract
- 2 tbsp butter, melted
- 1 package pie crust (or homemade)

Instructions:

1. Preheat oven to 350°F (175°C).
2. In a large bowl, whisk together the corn syrup, sugar, eggs, salt, vanilla, and melted butter until smooth.
3. Stir in the pecans.
4. Pour the mixture into the pie crust.
5. Bake for 50-55 minutes, or until the filling is set and golden brown.
6. Let cool before serving.

Peach Pie

Ingredients:

- 5-6 cups fresh peaches, peeled and sliced
- 1 cup granulated sugar
- 2 tbsp cornstarch
- 1/2 tsp ground cinnamon
- 1 tbsp lemon juice
- 2 tbsp butter, cut into small pieces
- 1 package pie crust (or homemade)

Instructions:

1. Preheat oven to 425°F (220°C).
2. In a large bowl, toss the peaches with sugar, cornstarch, cinnamon, and lemon juice.
3. Roll out the bottom pie crust and place it in a pie pan.
4. Pour the peach mixture into the crust and dot with butter.
5. Cover with the top crust, sealing the edges and making slits for ventilation.
6. Bake for 40-45 minutes until the crust is golden and the filling is bubbling.
7. Let cool before serving.

Chocolate Cream Pie

Ingredients:

- 1 package pie crust (or homemade)
- 2 cups whole milk
- 1 cup heavy cream
- 3/4 cup granulated sugar
- 1/2 cup unsweetened cocoa powder
- 1/4 tsp salt
- 3 large egg yolks
- 2 tbsp cornstarch
- 2 tbsp butter
- 1 tsp vanilla extract
- Whipped cream for topping (optional)

Instructions:

1. Preheat oven to 350°F (175°C) and bake the pie crust until golden, about 15 minutes. Let it cool.
2. In a saucepan, combine milk, cream, sugar, cocoa powder, and salt. Heat over medium, whisking constantly.
3. In a separate bowl, whisk the egg yolks and cornstarch until smooth. Gradually add a small amount of the hot milk mixture to the egg yolks, whisking constantly, to temper the eggs.
4. Pour the egg mixture back into the saucepan and cook, whisking constantly, until thickened.
5. Remove from heat and stir in the butter and vanilla extract.
6. Pour the chocolate filling into the cooled pie crust and refrigerate for at least 4 hours to set.
7. Top with whipped cream and serve.

Key Lime Pie

Ingredients:

- 1 1/2 cups graham cracker crumbs
- 1/4 cup sugar
- 1/2 cup unsalted butter, melted
- 3 large egg yolks
- 1 can (14 oz) sweetened condensed milk
- 1/2 cup key lime juice (fresh or bottled)
- 1 tbsp lime zest
- Whipped cream for topping (optional)

Instructions:

1. Preheat oven to 350°F (175°C).
2. In a bowl, combine graham cracker crumbs, sugar, and melted butter. Press mixture into the bottom of a pie dish to form the crust.
3. Bake for 10 minutes, then remove from oven and let cool.
4. In a separate bowl, whisk together egg yolks, sweetened condensed milk, key lime juice, and lime zest until smooth.
5. Pour the filling into the cooled crust and bake for 15 minutes.
6. Allow the pie to cool to room temperature, then refrigerate for at least 3 hours.
7. Top with whipped cream before serving.

Strawberry Rhubarb Pie

Ingredients:

- 2 cups strawberries, hulled and sliced
- 2 cups rhubarb, chopped
- 1 1/2 cups granulated sugar
- 1/4 cup cornstarch
- 1/4 tsp ground cinnamon
- 1 tbsp lemon juice
- 1 package pie crust (or homemade)

Instructions:

1. Preheat oven to 425°F (220°C).
2. In a bowl, mix strawberries, rhubarb, sugar, cornstarch, cinnamon, and lemon juice.
3. Roll out the bottom crust and fit it into a pie pan.
4. Pour the strawberry-rhubarb mixture into the crust.
5. Roll out the top crust and place it over the pie. Seal the edges and make slits for ventilation.
6. Bake for 40-45 minutes, until the crust is golden and the filling is bubbling.
7. Let cool before serving.

Sweet Potato Pie

Ingredients:

- 2 cups mashed sweet potatoes (about 2 medium potatoes)
- 1 cup heavy cream
- 3/4 cup granulated sugar
- 1/2 cup brown sugar
- 2 large eggs
- 1 tsp vanilla extract
- 1/2 tsp ground cinnamon
- 1/4 tsp ground nutmeg
- 1/4 tsp ground ginger
- 1 package pie crust (or homemade)

Instructions:

1. Preheat oven to 350°F (175°C).
2. In a bowl, combine mashed sweet potatoes, heavy cream, granulated sugar, brown sugar, eggs, vanilla, cinnamon, nutmeg, and ginger. Mix until smooth.
3. Pour the sweet potato filling into the prepared pie crust.
4. Bake for 55-60 minutes, or until the filling is set.
5. Let cool before serving.

Coconut Cream Pie

Ingredients:

- 1 1/2 cups sweetened shredded coconut
- 1 1/2 cups whole milk
- 1 cup heavy cream
- 3/4 cup granulated sugar
- 3 large egg yolks
- 1/4 cup cornstarch
- 1 tsp vanilla extract
- 1 package pie crust (or homemade)
- Whipped cream for topping

Instructions:

1. Preheat oven to 350°F (175°C) and bake the pie crust until golden, about 10-12 minutes. Let cool.
2. In a saucepan, combine coconut, milk, cream, and sugar. Heat over medium, stirring occasionally.
3. In a separate bowl, whisk egg yolks and cornstarch together. Gradually add a small amount of the hot milk mixture to temper the egg yolks.
4. Return the egg mixture to the saucepan and cook, whisking constantly, until thickened.
5. Remove from heat and stir in vanilla extract.
6. Pour the filling into the cooled pie crust and refrigerate for 2-3 hours.
7. Top with whipped cream and toasted coconut before serving.

Banana Cream Pie

Ingredients:

- 1 1/2 cups heavy cream
- 1/2 cup whole milk
- 3/4 cup granulated sugar
- 2 tbsp cornstarch
- 3 large egg yolks
- 1 tsp vanilla extract
- 2 ripe bananas, sliced
- 1 package pie crust (or homemade)
- Whipped cream for topping

Instructions:

1. Preheat oven to 350°F (175°C) and bake the pie crust until golden, about 10-12 minutes. Let cool.
2. In a saucepan, combine heavy cream, milk, sugar, and cornstarch. Heat over medium, whisking occasionally.
3. In a separate bowl, whisk the egg yolks. Gradually pour the hot milk mixture into the yolks while whisking to temper them.
4. Return the egg mixture to the saucepan and cook, whisking constantly, until thickened.
5. Remove from heat and stir in vanilla extract.
6. Layer sliced bananas in the cooled pie crust and pour the cream filling over them.
7. Refrigerate for at least 3 hours before serving. Top with whipped cream before serving.

Mixed Berry Pie

Ingredients:

- 2 cups strawberries, hulled and sliced
- 1 cup blueberries
- 1 cup raspberries
- 1 cup blackberries
- 3/4 cup granulated sugar
- 2 tbsp cornstarch
- 1 tbsp lemon juice
- 1/4 tsp ground cinnamon
- 1 package pie crust (or homemade)

Instructions:

1. Preheat oven to 425°F (220°C).
2. In a large bowl, mix together the berries, sugar, cornstarch, lemon juice, and cinnamon.
3. Roll out the bottom crust and place it in a pie dish.
4. Pour the berry mixture into the crust.
5. Roll out the top crust and cover the pie. Seal the edges and cut slits for ventilation.
6. Bake for 40-45 minutes, until the crust is golden and the filling is bubbly.
7. Let cool before serving.

Apple Cranberry Pie

Ingredients:

- 4 cups apples, peeled and sliced
- 1 1/2 cups fresh or frozen cranberries
- 3/4 cup granulated sugar
- 1/4 cup brown sugar
- 2 tbsp cornstarch
- 1/2 tsp ground cinnamon
- 1 tbsp lemon juice
- 1 package pie crust (or homemade)

Instructions:

1. Preheat oven to 375°F (190°C).
2. In a large bowl, mix together the apples, cranberries, sugars, cornstarch, cinnamon, and lemon juice.
3. Roll out the bottom crust and fit it into a pie pan.
4. Pour the apple-cranberry mixture into the pie.
5. Roll out the top crust and place it over the pie. Seal the edges and cut slits for ventilation.
6. Bake for 45-50 minutes, until the crust is golden and the filling is bubbly.
7. Let cool before serving.

Caramel Pecan Pie

Ingredients:

- 1 1/2 cups pecan halves
- 1/2 cup brown sugar
- 1/2 cup granulated sugar
- 1/2 cup unsalted butter, melted
- 1/4 cup heavy cream
- 3 large eggs
- 1 tsp vanilla extract
- 1 tbsp corn syrup
- 1 package pie crust (or homemade)

Instructions:

1. Preheat oven to 350°F (175°C).
2. In a bowl, combine brown sugar, granulated sugar, melted butter, heavy cream, eggs, vanilla, and corn syrup. Whisk until smooth.
3. Stir in the pecans.
4. Pour the mixture into the prepared pie crust.
5. Bake for 50-55 minutes, or until the filling is set and the crust is golden.
6. Let cool before serving.

Maple Walnut Pie

Ingredients:

- 1 1/2 cups walnuts, chopped
- 1/2 cup maple syrup
- 1/2 cup brown sugar
- 3 large eggs
- 1/4 cup unsalted butter, melted
- 1 tbsp vanilla extract
- 1 tbsp cornstarch
- 1 package pie crust (or homemade)

Instructions:

1. Preheat oven to 350°F (175°C).
2. In a bowl, whisk together maple syrup, brown sugar, eggs, melted butter, vanilla extract, and cornstarch.
3. Stir in the chopped walnuts.
4. Pour the filling into the pie crust.
5. Bake for 45-50 minutes, until the filling is set and the crust is golden.
6. Let cool before serving.

Pear Almond Pie

Ingredients:

- 4 ripe pears, peeled and sliced
- 1/2 cup almond flour
- 1/2 cup granulated sugar
- 1/4 cup unsalted butter, softened
- 2 large eggs
- 1 tsp almond extract
- 1 tbsp all-purpose flour
- 1/4 tsp ground cinnamon
- 1 package pie crust (or homemade)

Instructions:

1. Preheat oven to 375°F (190°C).
2. In a bowl, mix together almond flour, sugar, butter, eggs, almond extract, flour, and cinnamon until smooth.
3. Spread the almond filling in the bottom of the pie crust.
4. Arrange the pear slices on top of the almond filling.
5. Bake for 40-45 minutes, until the filling is golden and set.
6. Let cool before serving.

Rhubarb Pie

Ingredients:

- 4 cups rhubarb, chopped
- 1 1/2 cups granulated sugar
- 2 tbsp cornstarch
- 1 tbsp lemon juice
- 1/4 tsp ground cinnamon
- 1 package pie crust (or homemade)

Instructions:

1. Preheat oven to 425°F (220°C).
2. In a large bowl, combine rhubarb, sugar, cornstarch, lemon juice, and cinnamon. Mix until well combined.
3. Roll out the bottom crust and place it into a pie pan.
4. Pour the rhubarb mixture into the pie crust.
5. Roll out the top crust and place it over the pie. Seal the edges and cut slits for ventilation.
6. Bake for 40-45 minutes, until the crust is golden and the filling is bubbling.
7. Let cool before serving.

Buttermilk Pie

Ingredients:

- 1 1/2 cups granulated sugar
- 1/4 cup all-purpose flour
- 1/4 tsp salt
- 3 large eggs
- 1 cup buttermilk
- 1 tsp vanilla extract
- 1 tbsp unsalted butter, melted
- 1 package pie crust (or homemade)

Instructions:

1. Preheat oven to 350°F (175°C).
2. In a bowl, whisk together sugar, flour, salt, eggs, buttermilk, vanilla extract, and melted butter until smooth.
3. Pour the filling into the prepared pie crust.
4. Bake for 45-50 minutes, until the pie is golden and the filling is set.
5. Let cool before serving.

Chess Pie

Ingredients:

- 1 1/2 cups granulated sugar
- 2 tbsp cornmeal
- 1/4 tsp salt
- 3 large eggs
- 1/2 cup unsalted butter, melted
- 1 tbsp white vinegar
- 1 tsp vanilla extract
- 1/2 cup whole milk
- 1 package pie crust (or homemade)

Instructions:

1. Preheat oven to 350°F (175°C).
2. In a bowl, whisk together sugar, cornmeal, salt, eggs, melted butter, vinegar, vanilla extract, and milk until smooth.
3. Pour the filling into the prepared pie crust.
4. Bake for 45-50 minutes, until the pie is golden and the filling is set.
5. Let cool before serving.

Maple Pecan Pie

Ingredients:

- 1 1/2 cups pecans, chopped
- 1/2 cup maple syrup
- 1/2 cup brown sugar
- 3 large eggs
- 1/4 cup unsalted butter, melted
- 1 tsp vanilla extract
- 1 tbsp cornstarch
- 1 package pie crust (or homemade)

Instructions:

1. Preheat oven to 350°F (175°C).
2. In a bowl, whisk together maple syrup, brown sugar, eggs, melted butter, vanilla extract, and cornstarch.
3. Stir in the chopped pecans.
4. Pour the filling into the prepared pie crust.
5. Bake for 45-50 minutes, until the filling is set and the crust is golden.
6. Let cool before serving.

Lemon Custard Pie

Ingredients:

- 1 1/2 cups granulated sugar
- 1/4 cup all-purpose flour
- 1/4 tsp salt
- 3 large eggs
- 1 cup whole milk
- 1/2 cup fresh lemon juice
- 1 tbsp lemon zest
- 1 package pie crust (or homemade)

Instructions:

1. Preheat oven to 350°F (175°C).
2. In a bowl, whisk together sugar, flour, salt, eggs, milk, lemon juice, and lemon zest until smooth.
3. Pour the filling into the prepared pie crust.
4. Bake for 40-45 minutes, until the pie is golden and the filling is set.
5. Let cool before serving.

S'mores Pie

Ingredients:

- 1 1/2 cups graham cracker crumbs
- 1/4 cup granulated sugar
- 1/2 cup unsalted butter, melted
- 1 cup semisweet chocolate chips
- 1/2 cup heavy cream
- 1 1/2 cups mini marshmallows

Instructions:

1. Preheat oven to 350°F (175°C).
2. In a bowl, combine graham cracker crumbs, sugar, and melted butter. Press the mixture into the bottom of a pie dish to form the crust.
3. Bake the crust for 8-10 minutes, then remove from the oven and let cool.
4. In a saucepan, heat heavy cream over medium heat. Once hot, pour over the chocolate chips and stir until smooth to create the ganache.
5. Pour the ganache into the cooled pie crust.
6. Top with mini marshmallows and bake for 5-7 minutes, until the marshmallows are golden.
7. Let cool before serving.

Champagne Sorbet

Ingredients:

- **1 cup champagne or sparkling wine**
- **1/2 cup water**
- **1/2 cup sugar**
- **1 tablespoon lemon juice**

Instructions:

1. **Prepare the Syrup**
   In a saucepan, combine water and sugar. Heat over medium heat until the sugar dissolves, then remove from heat. Stir in the champagne and lemon juice.
2. **Freeze the Sorbet**
   Pour the mixture into an ice cream maker and churn according to the manufacturer's instructions. If you don't have an ice cream maker, pour the mixture into a shallow dish and freeze, stirring every 30 minutes until the sorbet reaches a slushy consistency.
3. **Serve**
   Scoop the sorbet into bowls or glasses and serve immediately.

Pistachio and Rose Water Baklava

Ingredients:

- 1 package phyllo dough
- 2 cups shelled pistachios, chopped
- 1/2 cup granulated sugar
- 1 teaspoon ground cinnamon
- 1 cup unsalted butter, melted
- 1 cup honey
- 1 tablespoon rose water

Instructions:

1. **Prepare the Filling**
   In a bowl, combine chopped pistachios, sugar, and cinnamon.
2. **Assemble the Baklava**
   Preheat the oven to 350°F (175°C). Brush a baking dish with melted butter and layer 6 sheets of phyllo dough, brushing each layer with butter. Sprinkle a thin layer of pistachio mixture over the dough. Repeat with 6 more sheets of phyllo and more pistachios. Continue layering and filling until all ingredients are used, finishing with 6 layers of phyllo dough on top.
3. **Cut and Bake**
   Cut the baklava into squares or diamonds and bake for 45-50 minutes, until golden and crispy.
4. **Make the Syrup**
   In a saucepan, combine honey and rose water. Heat gently, stirring until smooth, then pour over the hot baklava immediately after baking.
5. **Serve**
   Let the baklava cool to room temperature before serving.

Orange Almond Cake

Ingredients:

- 1 1/2 cups almond flour
- 1/2 cup all-purpose flour
- 1/2 teaspoon baking powder
- 1/4 teaspoon salt
- 1/2 cup unsalted butter, softened
- 1 cup sugar
- 3 large eggs
- Zest of 1 orange
- 1/4 cup fresh orange juice
- 1/2 teaspoon vanilla extract

Instructions:

1. **Prepare the Batter**
   Preheat the oven to 350°F (175°C). Grease and flour an 8-inch round cake pan. In a bowl, whisk together almond flour, all-purpose flour, baking powder, and salt.
2. **Cream the Butter and Sugar**
   In a separate bowl, beat the butter and sugar until light and fluffy. Add eggs one at a time, then stir in orange zest, orange juice, and vanilla extract.
3. **Combine and Bake**
   Gradually fold in the dry ingredients until just combined. Pour the batter into the prepared pan and bake for 30-35 minutes, or until a toothpick inserted comes out clean.
4. **Serve**
   Let the cake cool before removing from the pan and serving.

Dark Chocolate and Sea Salt Tart

Ingredients:

- 1 pre-baked tart crust
- 8 oz dark chocolate (70% cocoa), chopped
- 1/2 cup heavy cream
- 1 tablespoon unsalted butter
- 1/4 teaspoon sea salt

Instructions:

1. **Make the Ganache**
   In a saucepan, heat the heavy cream until it begins to simmer. Remove from heat and pour over the chopped chocolate. Let it sit for 2 minutes, then stir until smooth. Stir in the butter until fully incorporated.
2. **Fill the Tart**
   Pour the ganache into the pre-baked tart crust and smooth the top with a spatula.
3. **Chill and Garnish**
   Refrigerate the tart for at least 2 hours, until the ganache sets. Sprinkle with sea salt before serving.
4. **Serve**
   Slice the tart and enjoy!

Lemon and Thyme Olive Oil Cake

Ingredients:

- 1 1/2 cups all-purpose flour
- 1 teaspoon baking powder
- 1/2 teaspoon salt
- 1/2 cup extra virgin olive oil
- 1 cup sugar
- 3 large eggs
- Zest of 2 lemons
- 2 tablespoons fresh lemon juice
- 2 teaspoons fresh thyme leaves
- 1/2 cup whole milk

Instructions:

1. **Prepare the Batter**
   Preheat the oven to 350°F (175°C). Grease and flour a 9-inch cake pan. In a bowl, whisk together flour, baking powder, and salt.
2. **Mix Wet Ingredients**
   In another bowl, whisk together olive oil, sugar, eggs, lemon zest, lemon juice, and thyme until smooth.
3. **Combine and Bake**
   Gradually add the dry ingredients into the wet ingredients, alternating with milk, until fully combined. Pour the batter into the prepared pan and bake for 35-40 minutes, or until a toothpick comes out clean.
4. **Serve**
   Let the cake cool in the pan for 10 minutes, then remove and serve.

Matcha Chia Pudding

Ingredients:

- 1 tablespoon matcha powder
- 1 cup almond milk
- 2 tablespoons maple syrup
- 1/4 teaspoon vanilla extract
- 3 tablespoons chia seeds

Instructions:

1. **Make the Pudding**
   In a bowl, whisk together matcha powder, almond milk, maple syrup, and vanilla extract until smooth.
2. **Add Chia Seeds**
   Stir in chia seeds and mix well. Let the mixture sit for 5 minutes, then stir again.
3. **Chill**
   Cover and refrigerate for at least 4 hours or overnight, until the pudding thickens.
4. **Serve**
   Serve chilled, topped with fresh fruit or granola.

Cinnamon Sugar Churros with Chocolate Sauce

Ingredients:

- 1 cup water
- 1/4 cup unsalted butter
- 1 tablespoon sugar
- 1/2 teaspoon salt
- 1 cup all-purpose flour
- 2 large eggs
- 1 teaspoon vanilla extract
- 1/4 cup sugar (for coating)
- 1 teaspoon cinnamon (for coating)
- Vegetable oil for frying

Chocolate Sauce:

- 4 oz dark chocolate
- 1/2 cup heavy cream
- 1 tablespoon sugar

Instructions:

1. **Make the Churro Dough**
   In a saucepan, combine water, butter, sugar, and salt. Bring to a boil, then remove from heat. Stir in flour until smooth. Let the mixture cool for 5 minutes, then add eggs and vanilla extract, mixing until combined.
2. **Fry the Churros**
   Heat oil in a deep frying pan over medium-high heat. Fill a piping bag with the churro dough and pipe 4-inch lengths of dough into the hot oil. Fry until golden brown and crisp, about 2-3 minutes per side.
3. **Coat in Cinnamon Sugar**
   Combine sugar and cinnamon in a bowl. Remove the churros from the oil and coat them in the cinnamon sugar mixture.
4. **Make the Chocolate Sauce**
   Heat the cream in a saucepan until it begins to simmer, then pour over the chopped chocolate. Stir until smooth and add sugar to taste.
5. **Serve**
   Serve the churros with chocolate sauce for dipping.

Cherry Almond Galette

Ingredients:

- 1 sheet puff pastry
- 2 cups fresh cherries, pitted
- 1/4 cup sugar
- 1 tablespoon cornstarch
- 1/4 teaspoon almond extract
- 1 egg (for egg wash)
- Sliced almonds (for topping)

Instructions:

1. **Prepare the Filling**
   Preheat the oven to 375°F (190°C). In a bowl, toss cherries with sugar, cornstarch, and almond extract.
2. **Assemble the Galette**
   Roll out the puff pastry on a baking sheet lined with parchment paper. Spoon the cherry mixture into the center, leaving a border around the edges. Fold the edges over the cherries to form a rustic crust.
3. **Bake**
   Brush the edges of the pastry with an egg wash and sprinkle with sliced almonds. Bake for 35-40 minutes, or until the pastry is golden and the filling is bubbling.
4. **Serve**
   Let cool slightly before serving. Enjoy warm or at room temperature.

Pear Ginger Pie

Ingredients:

- 4-5 ripe pears, peeled and sliced
- 1/4 cup brown sugar
- 1 tablespoon ground ginger
- 1 teaspoon ground cinnamon
- 1/2 teaspoon ground nutmeg
- 1 tablespoon lemon juice
- 1 tablespoon cornstarch
- 1 tablespoon unsalted butter, cut into small pieces
- 1 package pie crust (or homemade)
- 1 egg (for egg wash)

Instructions:

1. **Prepare the Filling**
   Preheat the oven to 375°F (190°C). In a large bowl, combine the sliced pears with brown sugar, ginger, cinnamon, nutmeg, lemon juice, and cornstarch. Toss until the pears are evenly coated.

2. **Assemble the Pie**
   Roll out the pie crust and line a 9-inch pie dish. Fill with the pear mixture, then dot with butter pieces. Cover with the top pie crust, crimping the edges to seal. Cut a few slits in the top crust to allow steam to escape.

3. **Bake the Pie**
   Brush the top crust with an egg wash (whisked egg with a tablespoon of water) for a golden finish. Bake for 45-50 minutes, until the crust is golden brown and the filling is bubbly.

4. **Serve**
   Let the pie cool slightly before serving. Best enjoyed with a scoop of vanilla ice cream.

Raspberry Pie

Ingredients:

- **2 1/2 cups fresh raspberries**
- **1 cup sugar**
- **2 tablespoons cornstarch**
- **1 tablespoon lemon juice**
- **1 teaspoon vanilla extract**
- **1 package pie crust (or homemade)**
- **1 egg (for egg wash)**

Instructions:

1. **Prepare the Filling**
   Preheat the oven to 375°F (190°C). In a large bowl, mix raspberries, sugar, cornstarch, lemon juice, and vanilla extract until combined.
2. **Assemble the Pie**
   Roll out the pie crust and place it in a 9-inch pie dish. Pour the raspberry filling into the crust. Cover with the top crust, sealing the edges and cutting slits in the top to allow steam to escape.
3. **Bake the Pie**
   Brush the top crust with an egg wash for a golden finish. Bake for 40-45 minutes, until the crust is golden brown and the filling is bubbling.
4. **Serve**
   Cool the pie completely before serving. Enjoy with whipped cream or vanilla ice cream.

Triple Berry Pie

Ingredients:

- 1 cup strawberries, sliced
- 1 cup blueberries
- 1 cup blackberries
- 1 1/4 cups sugar
- 2 tablespoons cornstarch
- 1 tablespoon lemon juice
- 1 package pie crust (or homemade)
- 1 egg (for egg wash)

Instructions:

1. **Prepare the Filling**
   Preheat the oven to 375°F (190°C). In a large bowl, combine all the berries, sugar, cornstarch, and lemon juice, stirring gently to combine.
2. **Assemble the Pie**
   Roll out the pie crust and fit it into a 9-inch pie dish. Fill the crust with the berry mixture. Place the top crust on, sealing the edges and cutting slits for steam to escape.
3. **Bake the Pie**
   Brush the top crust with an egg wash for a golden finish. Bake for 40-45 minutes, until the crust is golden and the filling is bubbly.
4. **Serve**
   Let the pie cool before serving. A dollop of whipped cream or a scoop of vanilla ice cream complements it well.

Apricot Pie

Ingredients:

- 4 cups fresh apricots, pitted and sliced
- 1 cup sugar
- 2 tablespoons cornstarch
- 1 teaspoon lemon juice
- 1 teaspoon vanilla extract
- 1/2 teaspoon ground cinnamon
- 1 tablespoon unsalted butter, cut into small pieces
- 1 package pie crust (or homemade)

Instructions:

1. **Prepare the Filling**
   Preheat the oven to 375°F (190°C). In a large bowl, combine the apricots, sugar, cornstarch, lemon juice, vanilla extract, and cinnamon. Mix well.
2. **Assemble the Pie**
   Roll out the pie crust and line a 9-inch pie dish. Fill with the apricot mixture, then dot with butter pieces. Cover with the top pie crust, crimping the edges to seal, and cut a few slits in the top crust.
3. **Bake the Pie**
   Bake for 40-45 minutes, until the crust is golden and the filling is bubbly.
4. **Serve**
   Let the pie cool before serving. It's great on its own or with a scoop of vanilla ice cream.

Key Lime Coconut Pie

Ingredients:

- 1 1/2 cups sweetened shredded coconut
- 1 can (14 oz) sweetened condensed milk
- 1/2 cup fresh key lime juice
- 2 large eggs
- 1 tablespoon lime zest
- 1 pre-baked graham cracker crust

Instructions:

1. **Prepare the Filling**
   Preheat the oven to 350°F (175°C). In a bowl, whisk together the sweetened condensed milk, lime juice, eggs, and lime zest. Stir in the shredded coconut.
2. **Assemble the Pie**
   Pour the filling into the pre-baked graham cracker crust.
3. **Bake the Pie**
   Bake for 20-25 minutes, until the filling is set and slightly golden.
4. **Serve**
   Cool the pie completely before refrigerating for at least 2 hours. Serve chilled, garnished with extra coconut or whipped cream.

Apricot Almond Pie

Ingredients:

- 3 cups fresh apricots, pitted and sliced
- 1/2 cup slivered almonds
- 1 cup sugar
- 1 tablespoon cornstarch
- 1 teaspoon almond extract
- 1 tablespoon lemon juice
- 1 package pie crust (or homemade)

Instructions:

1. **Prepare the Filling**
   Preheat the oven to 375°F (190°C). In a large bowl, combine apricots, almonds, sugar, cornstarch, almond extract, and lemon juice.
2. **Assemble the Pie**
   Roll out the pie crust and fit it into a 9-inch pie dish. Pour the apricot mixture into the crust. Place the top crust over, sealing the edges and cutting slits for steam to escape.
3. **Bake the Pie**
   Bake for 40-45 minutes, until the crust is golden and the filling is bubbly.
4. **Serve**
   Cool the pie before serving. It pairs well with whipped cream or vanilla ice cream.

Sweet Lemon Pie

Ingredients:

- 1 can (14 oz) sweetened condensed milk
- 1/2 cup fresh lemon juice
- 2 large eggs
- 1 tablespoon lemon zest
- 1 pre-baked graham cracker crust

Instructions:

1. **Prepare the Filling**
   Preheat the oven to 350°F (175°C). In a bowl, whisk together the sweetened condensed milk, lemon juice, eggs, and lemon zest.
2. **Assemble the Pie**
   Pour the filling into the pre-baked graham cracker crust.
3. **Bake the Pie**
   Bake for 20-25 minutes, until the filling is set and lightly browned on top.
4. **Serve**
   Let the pie cool to room temperature, then refrigerate for at least 2 hours before serving.

Gingerbread Pie

Ingredients:

- 1 1/2 cups molasses
- 1 cup heavy cream
- 3/4 cup sugar
- 3 large eggs
- 1 tablespoon ground ginger
- 1 teaspoon ground cinnamon
- 1/2 teaspoon ground cloves
- 1/4 teaspoon ground nutmeg
- 1 pre-baked pie crust

Instructions:

1. **Prepare the Filling**
   Preheat the oven to 375°F (190°C). In a saucepan, combine molasses, heavy cream, and sugar. Heat gently until the sugar dissolves.
2. **Mix the Eggs and Spices**
   In a separate bowl, beat the eggs, then whisk in the ginger, cinnamon, cloves, and nutmeg.
3. **Combine and Bake**
   Gradually add the molasses mixture to the eggs, whisking constantly. Pour the mixture into the pre-baked pie crust.
4. **Bake the Pie**
   Bake for 35-40 minutes, until the filling is set and slightly firm to the touch.
5. **Serve**
   Cool before serving, and consider adding a dollop of whipped cream or a sprinkle of cinnamon.

Chocolate Pudding Pie

Ingredients:

- 1 pre-baked pie crust
- 2 cups whole milk
- 3/4 cup sugar
- 1/4 cup unsweetened cocoa powder
- 1/4 cup cornstarch
- 1/4 teaspoon salt
- 3 large egg yolks
- 2 tablespoons unsalted butter
- 1 teaspoon vanilla extract
- Whipped cream (for topping)

Instructions:

1. **Prepare the Pudding**
   In a medium saucepan, whisk together the milk, sugar, cocoa powder, cornstarch, and salt. Heat over medium heat, stirring constantly, until the mixture comes to a boil and thickens.
2. **Temper the Eggs**
   In a small bowl, whisk the egg yolks. Slowly pour about 1/2 cup of the hot milk mixture into the egg yolks while whisking to prevent curdling. Gradually add the egg yolk mixture back into the saucepan, whisking constantly.
3. **Finish the Pudding**
   Continue to cook for 2-3 minutes until the pudding is thick. Remove from heat and stir in the butter and vanilla extract.
4. **Assemble the Pie**
   Pour the pudding into the pre-baked pie crust and spread evenly. Chill in the refrigerator for at least 2 hours until set.
5. **Serve**
   Top with whipped cream and serve cold.

Baked Custard Pie

Ingredients:

- 1 pre-baked pie crust
- 3 large eggs
- 2 cups whole milk
- 3/4 cup sugar
- 1 teaspoon vanilla extract
- 1/4 teaspoon ground nutmeg
- Pinch of salt

Instructions:

1. **Prepare the Custard Mixture**
   Preheat the oven to 350°F (175°C). In a bowl, whisk the eggs and sugar together. Add the milk, vanilla, nutmeg, and a pinch of salt, and whisk until smooth.
2. **Assemble the Pie**
   Pour the custard mixture into the pre-baked pie crust.
3. **Bake the Pie**
   Bake for 45-50 minutes, or until the custard is set and lightly browned on top. A knife inserted into the center should come out clean.
4. **Serve**
   Allow the pie to cool completely before serving. A sprinkle of cinnamon or nutmeg on top adds a nice touch.

Walnut Pie

Ingredients:

- 1 pre-baked pie crust
- 1 1/2 cups chopped walnuts
- 3/4 cup light corn syrup
- 3/4 cup sugar
- 3 large eggs
- 1/4 cup unsalted butter, melted
- 1 teaspoon vanilla extract
- 1/4 teaspoon salt

Instructions:

1. **Prepare the Filling**
   Preheat the oven to 350°F (175°C). In a bowl, whisk together the corn syrup, sugar, eggs, melted butter, vanilla extract, and salt until smooth.
2. **Assemble the Pie**
   Pour the walnut pieces into the pre-baked pie crust, then pour the filling over the walnuts.
3. **Bake the Pie**
   Bake for 40-45 minutes, or until the filling is set and slightly puffed up.
4. **Serve**
   Let the pie cool before serving. It's great with a scoop of vanilla ice cream or whipped cream.

Apple Butter Pie

Ingredients:

- 1 pre-baked pie crust
- 1 cup apple butter
- 1/2 cup sugar
- 1 tablespoon cornstarch
- 1/2 teaspoon ground cinnamon
- 1/4 teaspoon ground nutmeg
- 1/4 teaspoon ground ginger
- 2 large eggs
- 1/2 cup heavy cream

Instructions:

1. **Prepare the Filling**
   Preheat the oven to 350°F (175°C). In a bowl, whisk together the apple butter, sugar, cornstarch, cinnamon, nutmeg, and ginger. Add the eggs and heavy cream, whisking until smooth.
2. **Assemble the Pie**
   Pour the filling into the pre-baked pie crust.
3. **Bake the Pie**
   Bake for 40-45 minutes, or until the filling is set and the crust is golden.
4. **Serve**
   Allow the pie to cool before serving. It pairs wonderfully with whipped cream.

Cider Pie

Ingredients:

- 1 pre-baked pie crust
- 2 cups apple cider (reduced to 1/2 cup)
- 3/4 cup sugar
- 3 tablespoons cornstarch
- 1/2 teaspoon ground cinnamon
- 1/4 teaspoon ground cloves
- 1/4 teaspoon ground nutmeg
- 3 large eggs
- 2 tablespoons unsalted butter, melted

Instructions:

1. **Prepare the Filling**
   In a saucepan, reduce the apple cider over medium heat until it thickens to about 1/2 cup. Remove from heat and set aside.
2. **Make the Custard**
   In a separate bowl, whisk together the sugar, cornstarch, cinnamon, cloves, and nutmeg. In another bowl, whisk the eggs. Gradually add the reduced cider and the egg mixture to the dry ingredients, whisking until smooth. Stir in the melted butter.
3. **Assemble the Pie**
   Pour the filling into the pre-baked pie crust.
4. **Bake the Pie**
   Bake at 350°F (175°C) for 40-45 minutes, until the filling is set.
5. **Serve**
   Let the pie cool before serving.

Caramel Apple Pie

Ingredients:

- 1 pre-baked pie crust
- 6 cups apples, peeled and sliced
- 1/2 cup caramel sauce
- 1 tablespoon lemon juice
- 3/4 cup sugar
- 2 tablespoons flour
- 1 teaspoon ground cinnamon
- 1/4 teaspoon ground nutmeg
- 1 tablespoon unsalted butter, cut into small pieces

Instructions:

1. **Prepare the Filling**
   Preheat the oven to 375°F (190°C). In a large bowl, toss the apple slices with caramel sauce and lemon juice. In a separate bowl, mix the sugar, flour, cinnamon, and nutmeg, then add this to the apples. Toss to coat.
2. **Assemble the Pie**
   Pour the apple filling into the pre-baked pie crust and dot with butter.
3. **Bake the Pie**
   Bake for 45-50 minutes, or until the apples are tender and the crust is golden brown.
4. **Serve**
   Let the pie cool before serving. A scoop of vanilla ice cream or whipped cream is a perfect addition.

Mincemeat Pie

Ingredients:

- 1 pre-baked pie crust
- 2 cups mincemeat filling (store-bought or homemade)
- 1/4 cup brandy or rum (optional)
- 1/2 cup sugar
- 1/2 teaspoon ground cinnamon
- 1/4 teaspoon ground allspice
- 1/4 teaspoon ground cloves
- 1 tablespoon lemon juice

Instructions:

1. **Prepare the Filling**
   Preheat the oven to 375°F (190°C). In a bowl, mix the mincemeat with the brandy or rum (if using), sugar, cinnamon, allspice, cloves, and lemon juice.
2. **Assemble the Pie**
   Pour the mincemeat filling into the pre-baked pie crust and cover with the top crust, sealing the edges and cutting slits for steam to escape.
3. **Bake the Pie**
   Bake for 45-50 minutes, or until the crust is golden brown.
4. **Serve**
   Allow the pie to cool before serving. It's traditionally served with whipped cream or hard sauce.

Raspberry Almond Pie

Ingredients:

- 1 pre-baked pie crust
- 2 cups fresh raspberries
- 1/2 cup sliced almonds
- 1 cup sugar
- 1 tablespoon cornstarch
- 1 teaspoon almond extract
- 1/4 teaspoon salt
- 1 tablespoon unsalted butter, cut into small pieces

Instructions:

1. **Prepare the Filling**
   Preheat the oven to 375°F (190°C). In a large bowl, toss the raspberries with sugar, cornstarch, almond extract, and salt.
2. **Assemble the Pie**
   Pour the raspberry filling into the pre-baked pie crust. Sprinkle the sliced almonds over the top and dot with butter.
3. **Bake the Pie**
   Bake for 35-40 minutes, or until the filling is bubbling and the crust is golden.
4. **Serve**
   Let the pie cool before serving. A scoop of vanilla ice cream is a great addition.

Pumpkin Pecan Pie

Ingredients:

- 1 pre-baked pie crust
- 1 1/2 cups pumpkin puree
- 3/4 cup light corn syrup
- 3/4 cup packed brown sugar
- 3 large eggs
- 1/4 cup melted butter
- 1 teaspoon ground cinnamon
- 1/2 teaspoon ground ginger
- 1/4 teaspoon ground nutmeg
- 1/2 teaspoon salt
- 1 cup chopped pecans

Instructions:

1. **Prepare the Filling**
   Preheat the oven to 375°F (190°C). In a bowl, combine pumpkin puree, corn syrup, brown sugar, eggs, melted butter, cinnamon, ginger, nutmeg, and salt. Stir until smooth.
2. **Assemble the Pie**
   Pour the filling into the pre-baked pie crust. Sprinkle the chopped pecans over the top.
3. **Bake the Pie**
   Bake for 50-55 minutes, or until the filling is set and the pecans are toasted.
4. **Serve**
   Let the pie cool completely before serving.

Lemon Blueberry Pie

Ingredients:

- 1 pre-baked pie crust
- 2 cups fresh blueberries
- 1/2 cup sugar
- 1/4 cup cornstarch
- 1/2 teaspoon lemon zest
- 2 tablespoons fresh lemon juice
- 1/4 teaspoon salt
- 1 tablespoon butter

Instructions:

1. **Prepare the Filling**
   Preheat the oven to 375°F (190°C). In a saucepan, mix the blueberries, sugar, cornstarch, lemon zest, lemon juice, and salt. Cook over medium heat until the mixture thickens and the berries burst.
2. **Assemble the Pie**
   Pour the blueberry filling into the pre-baked pie crust. Dot with butter.
3. **Bake the Pie**
   Bake for 30-35 minutes, or until the filling is bubbly and the crust is golden brown.
4. **Serve**
   Let the pie cool completely before serving.

www.ingramcontent.com/pod-product-compliance
Lightning Source LLC
Chambersburg PA
CBHW080355040225
21332CB00047B/1660